"Treat the earth well.
It was not given to you by your parents,
it was loaned to you by your children.
We do not inherit the Earth from our Ancestors,
we borrow it from our Children."
~ Ancient Indian Proverb ~

Haji's Fight for Freedom

Nature's Guardians Series Book 1

by
Alisha M. Risen-Kent

Dedication

For my children, who are my strength and motivation; my
whole world.
For my parents, who always believed in my dream.
For my beta and best friend, without whom I would have never
found the courage to write this.
Lastly, to all my family and friends who encouraged me along
the way.

Table of Contents

Chapter One: Beginnings   1

Chapter Two: On Our Own   9

Chapter Three: Alone   16

Chapter Four: Going Home   26

Conservation Efforts   32

Timber's Gambit (excerpt)   34

Chapter One: Beginnings

The first memory I have is of the blinding light that pierced the crack in my egg as I pushed against the thin shell. The sun's excruciating rays penetrated my sensitive eyes, and I pulled back within the relative comfort of my sanctuary. I didn't want to go back out, but something stronger than my will urged me forward, and I pushed out into the world.

My shell rolled away as I fell onto the rough floor of my nest. My body shivered, the moisture from my wet feathers chilling me to the bone. My first experience of the world left me wishing I had never left my egg. But soon, my siblings joined me, greeting the new world in the same fashion as I. We cuddled together for warmth, our tiny bodies shaking in tandem. We were not alone for long.

A shadow fell over the nest, and we glanced up to see what new challenge sat before us. Our mother smiled down, as well as any bird could, her eyes aglow with love and affection. She bent her head to mine and filled my gullet. I hadn't even been aware how hungry I was until that moment. The morsel gave me strength and as she pulled away, I cried for more, as did my two siblings who went without.

She flapped her large wings once and disappeared. For the rest of that day, both she and my father brought food for my siblings and I until we were fat and sated. As the sun sank to the horizon, both returned to the nest. I caught a glimpse of my father, perched proud and regal, on a branch nearby before my mother lowered her bulk over us, the feathers of her breast parting and engulfing us within their warmth.

Over the next several days, we settled into a routine. My parents left as the sun rose, spending all day collecting tidbits of food and bringing them to us, and as the sun set, they would settle down and sleep. Perhaps if I had understood things a bit better, I could have prevented what happened next.

When my sister had emerged from her egg, my brother and I dwarfed her. So, when my parents brought food, more often than not, she couldn't reach the beak that bent down to deliver it. In my hunger, I never considered the consequence of this. After a few days, she simply quit trying and only gave a weak cry. Still, once our parents left, we went back to huddling close together.

Looking back, I think my mother may have known something was wrong, either from experience or just mother's intuition. When she returned at night, she spent a little more time showing my sister affection. But it was little comfort in the end.

A week or so after we emerged, my sister had become too weak to cuddle with us and just lay on her side at the bottom of the nest. I cried softly to her, knowing if she stayed there, she would freeze. But no answer came forth. When next my mother approached the nest, I cried to her while she fed my brother. She turned sad eyes to me and followed my gaze. In what seemed a cruel act to me, she picked up my sister and threw her from the nest. I balked at my mother, not understanding that my sister had already died. Later, I came to understand the deep anguish my mother suffered at the loss of her child.

The next several weeks, my brother and I grew quickly. I proved stronger and slightly bigger and often teased him when our parents were away. He played along most of the time, saying that, yeah, I may be bigger, but he was smarter. I gave him that one. I preferred exploring to studying and this often got me into trouble.

My juvenile feathers had begun to push past the soft downy, and I itched to take to the sky. The long feathers needed for flight gave me a gangly appearance, especially with the absence of crucial tail feathers. But it didn't stop me. I would often hop to the end of the branch where our nest lay and work the muscles of my back. Downy feathers rained down, evidence of my disobedience, and my father would scold me… again.

One time, while doing this, I tried to get my brother to join me.

"Come on, Koru," I cried. "How are you ever going to learn to fly if you spend all day cooped up in the nest?"

"I will learn when the time is right, Haji," he said, patient as ever. "What are you going to do if you slip and fall?"

"I won't. I know exactly what I'm doing."

And with that, I started out toward the branch again. I didn't get very far, however, as my father dropped down in front of me. He sighed and shook his head.

"Since you're so eager, Haji, how about your first lesson," he said, turning and heading down the branch.

"Father!" Koru yelled. "Are you sure that's a good idea? Haji doesn't even have all of his feathers yet."

I ignored him and bounded after my father, who simply waved at the concerned Koru. My brother sat back and watched anxiously. I glanced at him over my shoulder and noticed a look in his eyes I didn't expect: Desire. He wished to learn just as badly as I did, but his fear held him back. I thought if I could make it look easy, he wouldn't be so scared anymore.

"Now, the first thing you have to remember is balance," my father began. "Hold your wings out without moving them until you can balance without tipping."

Well, this'll be easy, I thought. I did as instructed and stretched my wings wide, but balancing was easier said than done. The wind, even though mostly calm, still managed to tip my wings one way or the other. After some time, I learned the best way to compensate for it and no longer risked falling.

"Okay, good," my father said, pleased with my progress. "Time for a quick lesson in aerodynamics. In order to fly, you can't just flap your wings up and down. That's probably why your back has been hurting you. You need to roll your shoulders forward and under, where the end of your flight feathers nearly touch in front of your beak. I'll show you."

He hopped a step back and flapped his wings in slow motion.

"This way, you're pushing the air behind you instead of underneath you," he continued. "You'll use a lot less energy that way. Go ahead and try it."

I did as he said and, a bit overzealous in my attempt, nearly tipped over, the roaring from the wind deafening to my ears. But I had lifted up several inches and tittered with excitement.

"Very good, Haji," my father praised. "With practice, you'll learn to move silently, something our species needs in order to survive. If you make too much noise, you won't be able to hunt."

"I understand, Father," I said, and followed him back to the nest.

Koru still stared out at us, and I noticed an unmistakable gleam in his eye. He had put away the lesson Father had taught me. I would not have been surprised if Koru mastered flying on his first try simply by having watched father and me. Mother returned home then, carrying a large rabbit. We ate well that night. A week later, everything changed in my life.

Chapter Two: On Our Own

I spent the next week practicing my flying and even managed to get Koru to follow me to the end of the branch. He watched as I successfully flew up to the next branch and back down again. My landing proved less than perfect, but he shivered in excitement none the less. I watched as he prepared to follow my example, his wings opened wide in anticipation. Just as they came down for the first time, Mother swooped up from underneath us, smacking Koru and I in the head with her talons. It hurt, and I made to cry out when I noticed the look of fright in her eyes.

"Come, boys!" she called, diving for the nest.

We didn't hesitate and followed her example, attempting to hide with her in the tight quarters. I felt like an eyas again and wanted to ask her what had frightened her. Then I heard it, the loud baying of an animal I'd never seen nor heard before. The sound sent chills down my spine, and I felt Koru shivering next to me.

"Mother," I asked, softly. "What is that?"

At first, she didn't answer. After a minute of worried glances in the trees, she turned to me. "They are dogs, son. But they are not what you should fear."

"What is it, then, that I should fear?" I began to shiver as well at the tone of her voice. I couldn't imagine anything that could scare my strong mother.

"It is the creatures that walk with them," she said, turning her eyes back to the trees. "They walk on two legs, like us, but they do not respect the forest as we do. They carry fire in long tubes that can reach far away. Even we, who live in the sky, are not safe. Too many of your kin have fallen prey to their weapons."

I tucked back under her wing, trying to drown out the sound of the dogs as they moved closer. Several minutes passed before a horrible thought occurred to me. I poked my head back out and looked up again.

"Mother!" I whispered fiercely, the dogs too near to speak normally. "Where is father?"

She didn't answer, but I saw, for one moment, her unguarded expression. She worried for him as well. Suddenly a loud crack echoed the forest, louder than the thunder during a storm. All three of us jumped. A faint cry echoed back, full of fear and pain. I didn't want to admit that I recognized the cry. But I felt my mother tense and then begin to shiver like Koru and me. I can't begin to describe how my rock-solid foundation shook with the knowledge that my mother had fallen apart.

In time, the baying hounds disappeared, as did the creatures that followed them. Darkness fell but father never returned. If birds could cry, we would have. My mother and Koru trembled through the night, trying to suppress emotions we all felt. I did my best to remain strong for them, especially Koru, who looked up to father more than anyone. The next morning, Mother left without a word. Koru still mourned and refused to leave the tight ball he'd rolled himself in to. I tried to pull him out of it.

"Come on, Koru," I pled. "We have to be strong for mother. She needs us now."

"How can I be strong for someone else when I can't even be strong for myself? He never even taught me how to fly."

"Don't be like this," I said, nudging him with my beak. "We both know you can probably fly better than me."

A sudden movement caught my attention and I looked up to see Mother returning with a squirrel. It surprised me that she'd returned so early. She dropped the rodent in the nest and flew up to a higher perch. I looked up at her, concerned. The squirrel could've fed all of us, but she did not join Koru and I. Even Koru hesitated.

"I don't understand," I said aloud.

Koru glanced up at me, a small piece of meat disappearing into his mouth.

"What?" he asked.

"Mother isn't eating. I wonder if she's going to be all right."

Koru looked up at her as well, his sadness coming back. "I don't know. Dad once said that our kind mate for life." He turned back down to his food. "We should probably just leave her alone for now and eat the food she brought for us. Without father, she's going to have to work twice as hard to feed us."

"You're right," I said, looking away from my mourning mother and joining Koru.

After we finished the squirrel, my mother called for me. With some effort, I flew up to her branch.

"Can you fly well enough to hunt on your own," she asked, looking at something only she could see.

"I believe so," I answered.

"Can you teach Koru?"

"I believe Koru already knows but lacks the confidence to try." I tried to decipher her cryptic questions, to no avail.

Without warning, she swooped off the branch, dislodging me from my precarious perch. To my ultimate horror, she dived down at the unsuspecting Koru. I couldn't even call out a warning before she crashed into him, knocking him from the nest. Koru screamed in terror, flapping his wings uselessly as he fell toward the ground. I dived after him, knowing there was very little I could actually do.

"Turn over, Koru!" I called. "You can do this! I know you can."

He closed his eyes and flipped over, flapping his wings with all his might. I squealed in excitement as he righted himself and hovered in mid-air.

"You did it!" I cried, flying around him.

He opened his eyes and looked around. "I guess I did."

"Ha! You're a natural, just like I said you'd be."

"Yeah," he said, turning a summersault. "But… why"

We both looked up just in time to see our mother disappear through the trees.

"Koru, I think we're on our own," I said.

"I think you're right," he agreed.

Chapter Three: Alone

For the next several months, we stuck close together, using the nest our parents left for us and hunted as one. I dreaded the day we would go our separate ways, the loneliness that would follow always at the front of my mind. When the time came, however, Koru's happiness overcame everything else. A pretty little hen had attracted his attention. It surprised me because Koru always seemed so quiet and reserved. When he saw her, his eyes shone like our parents' had, and I encouraged him to seek the hen out. She accepted him right away. And who wouldn't? Koru personified perfection. So, I went my own way, promising to check in on him in a year or two.

Several more months passed, and I settled into a routine of sorts. I stayed close to home, not having any reason to leave. Hunting proved fruitful and for the most part, it was quiet. Every now and then, I would run into Kuro or his mate. Not long after leaving together, they produced a family of their own, two males and a female. I delighted in meeting the little ones and watched as they grew and took to the sky themselves. Then, a year after my father had been killed, I once again heard the baying of the hounds.

I had ventured quite far from the nest and the nearness of the hounds surprised me. Trying to make it back to my sanctuary, I weaved through the trees as silently as I could. But in my panic, I couldn't see the man-animals hiding in the undergrowth. The forest echoed the crack of their weapon, louder than I'd ever heard, and a sudden pain assaulted my wing. I screamed and stumbled in my flight, my mangled limb useless. The branches below me broke my fall, and I tumbled, head over tail to the ground.

The baying echoed in my ears, and I clenched my beak against the pain. They were so close! If not for the thick undergrowth, I'm sure they would have found me. I was grateful Koru had settled deeper in the forest. At least he and his family would be safe. In time, the hounds and their masters drifted away. My hiding spot kept me from being discovered.

Hours later, once I was sure the man-animals were gone, I stumbled from the undergrowth. I knew the dangers of staying on the ground but could not reach the safety of the trees. Flapping my wings left me with an excruciating pain, and I resigned to traveling along the forest floor.

"Maybe it will heal," I said to myself.

But I knew the likelihood of surviving that long. Without the ability to fly, I couldn't hunt. Yet, I refused to give up. I'd come too far to die on the ground.

I'm not sure how far I stumbled with my wing dragging behind me, but the sun had set when I became too exhausted to continue. I lay there that night, the sounds that usually went unnoticed bringing new fears to my already anxiety-ridden body. Not expecting to survive the night, it surprised me when the morning sun woke me from my troubled slumber. Still too weak to move, I lay sprawled across the forest floor, the sun's rays trying valiantly to reach me through the canopy.

Sometime that day, a noise reached me through the fog of my mind. I couldn't pinpoint it at first, and I feared that more than anything. Then it appeared before me, a man-animal. I screeched in anger and fear, hoping to scare the creature off. Of course, I didn't. The creature towered over me, many times my size. Despite my threat, it came at me cautiously but unafraid. My sharp beak and talons were no match for the thick gloves covering its arms.

"You poor thing," she said, even though I couldn't understand her speech. "This happens every year."

She reached down and picked me up, cradling me to her chest. My wing screamed in protest, as did I, but she pulled something over my eyes. The darkness calmed me, and my screeches of protest became soft cries of pain. A short while later, I found myself in a large enclosure, the mesh ceiling a mockery of freedom. A splint held my wing immobile and, although uncomfortable, it eased the pain of the break. Homesick and trapped, I lifted my head and cried. I worried for Koru and his family and feared I would never see them again.

For several days, I stared up at the mesh screen that covered my enclosure. Pulling in a lungful of air, I flapped my wings furiously in an attempt to leave the perch I rested on. My bandaged wing refused to hold my weight and buckled under the strain. Resigned, I fell back on my haunches, panting from exertion. My eyes strayed again to the sky. If only I were stronger, I could tear the mesh and regain my freedom. Or if I were smaller, I could simply squeeze through it. Sighing, I settled for watching other birds flying free above me. How I missed the sky!

Sixty sunrises passed there as I healed. Although everything I needed was provided for me, like food, water and shelter, I still ached to fly free. I missed my home and feared Koru would worry and come looking for me. Another part of me wished he would. Surely Koru could figure out some way of freeing me. With the pain in my wing gone, I knew I could fly free once the bandage was removed.

I often heard the man-animals talking and acquired a rudimentary understanding of their language. One man-animal in particular, Jess, they called her, took a liking to me. She spoke in long-winded and one-sided conversations, never trying to reach out and touch me as many of the other man-animals did. I refused to speak back to her. But her calming voice lulled me into a sense of complacency, and I found I didn't mind her company.

"Udugi, how are you today?" Jess. She had given me a different name. She told me once that it meant hope in an ancient language of her people. "We are going to take that bandage off your wing. Are you ready to be free of it?"

Of course, I can't answer you. But yes, I'd gladly have the cumbersome object removed, I answered in my head.

"Will you come to me?"

This is a first, but I suppose. You have never given me reason to distrust you.

I hopped along the makeshift perch toward the tidbit of meat in her hand, bringing to mind the days of my youth when I first learned to fly. Jess held her arm out and, with a great leap, I landed on her gloved forearm. I wondered briefly where we were going as she led me from my cage. There were man-animals everywhere, and I began to panic.

"Shhh," Jess cooed in my ear, calming me. "We're nearly there."

She pushed through a door and entered into a bright room. I remembered the room from when I first arrived at the sanctuary. They'd brought me there while working on my wing. Another man-animal, the same one who usually tended to my wound, approached.

"How is he today, Jess?" he asked, reaching for my wing.

"Quite calm, actually. I'm a bit surprised he came to me so willingly."

"Are you thinking of keeping him with us?" the doctor asked.

"Not if he can fly and hunt on his own. He needs to go back where he belongs. I think I will show him this weekend and then see about returning him home."

The doctor removed the bandage and prodded at the bone. I turned my head and bumped his hand with my beak. His prodding didn't hurt, but I disliked him touching my wing. Ignoring my protests, he stretched and folded it, checking the flexibility.

"Well, it looks like his wing made a full recovery."

With the weight removed, I flapped my wings experimentally. It felt like heaven and, if not for the string attached to my foot, I would have flown around the room. I noticed both Jess and the doctor laughing and discontinued my action, my wings open but stationary. Jess offered me her arm again, and I took it without hesitation. Together, we returned to my enclosure, and Jess released the string on my foot.

I couldn't wait to be free of the restraint. Even if I couldn't leave my enclosure, I could at least fly around in it, and flying anywhere was better than not flying at all. As soon as I felt the string loosen, I took to the air. Oh, how I'd missed the feeling of wind beneath my wings! I sensed Jess' happiness and found it contagious. Without a word, she slipped from the aviary. Unused to the exercise, I tired easily, and when I landed on my perch, I noticed she had disappeared. I sighed with contentment, joy replacing the emptiness in my heart.

Chapter Four: Going Home

A week later, with my wings as good as new, Jess carried me out of my enclosure and into a holding pen with other birds.

"Welcome again to our Birds of Prey show," an announcer called from outside the pen.

Jess sat across from me, but it did little to assuage my nervousness. Other birds from the sanctuary rested nearby, some anxious like me, and others old pros. An old eagle with half of one of his wings missing, tried to calm my fears. He had been in the show for half his life.

"What happened to your wing?" I asked.

"Same as you, I suspect," he answered. "Only I wasn't as lucky."

I sympathized with the old eagle, trying to imagine myself never being able to fly again. My heart hurt for him, and I turned away. Even now, the sky called to me. I thought about Koru and his family. His younglings would have fledged by now and possibly even started families of their own. I wondered, for the first time, if I would ever have the chance to find a mate and have a family. Turning back to the old eagle, I found him watching me with a knowing look on his face.

"Did you have a family?" I asked.

"Yes," he answered, closing his eyes.

"Do you miss them?"

"Yes. My eaglets were near fledging when I lost my wing. I'm sure they have their own families now. My mate is strong and, although I worry for her, I believe she is doing well."

I remained silent for a moment, thinking of my own parents. For the first time in more than two years, I thought about my mother. Neither Koru nor I had seen her since she left us.

"My father died just before my brother and I fledged," I said, looking up at the sky. "My mother left us soon after. I worried for her but she, like your mate, is strong. Do you think she was able to start a new life with a new mate?"

"I imagine so, young falcon," the old eagle said.

"Do eagles have the same mate their whole lives?"

"Yes, unless one mate dies. In that case, the surviving eagle seeks a new companion. I suspect your mother did the same."

"That makes me happy. I can't imagine her being sad and alone forever."

"Fear not, Haji. The humans will take you home soon, and you will have your chance. Healthy birds are always brought home." Closing his eyes, the old eagle snuggled his white head into the brown feathers of his chest.

I began to have a newfound appreciation for my position. My wing had completely healed, and I would be able to return to my forest. Jess turned to me then and smiled.

"Are you ready, Udugi?" she asked and held her arm out to me. I settled my bulk on her glove and she made her way to the stage.

"This is Udugi," the head of the sanctuary called. "He is one of the many birds of prey that are shot down each year. But he is lucky and will be able to return to his home. Say hi, Udugi."

Jess prompted me to open my wings, and I did so proudly, the crowd of man-animals clapping in response. The mood went to my head a bit, and I screeched out a greeting. Jess smiled and gave me a piece of meat. A few moments later, we were back inside the building.

"You were very good today," Jess said, running her finger down my back. "I'm really going to miss you."

A couple days later, I understood what she meant. She collected me from my enclosure and carried me to the doctor. He fastened a colorful band on my leg and then placed me in a tiny cage. Jess stayed by me the whole time, but it did little to ease my anxiety. An eternity later, the vehicle we were in came to a stop and the man-animals disembarked. Jess retrieved my tiny carrier and walked a little distance away. I could already smell the familiar scents of my home, and I became excited.

Jess removed the cloth that covered my cage and flipped up the locks. In one swift motion, she lifted the lid. Even before it had been completely removed, I sprang into action, my wings beating furiously as I took to the sky. In my joy, I called out a greeting and the forest welcomed me home. I noticed Jess standing at the edge of the forest, a smile stretched across her face. I swooped past her, the wind from my fly-by mussing her hair. Her laughter echoed in my ears as I disappeared into the trees.

To my everlasting joy, Koru heard my call, and he and his mate met me near our old nest. We spent a moment summersaulting around each other. I was free, and I was home.

LAST CHANCE FOREVER
The Bird of Prey Conservancy

Conservation Efforts

Every year, hundreds of birds of prey are ruthlessly injured or killed, leading many to be threatened or endangered. In addition, other man-made hazards affect the mortality of these majestic creatures. Some of these are pollution from pesticides or oil, lead poisoning, and ingestion of poisons by eating infected prey. Another area of concern is electrocution. Raptors perch on power lines for hunting, roosting, and nesting. Up to 90% of raptor deaths are caused from electrocution, most of these involving young eagles ("Birds of Prey"). Although it is now illegal to shoot birds of prey, they were once hunted for sport or to keep them from competing for natural food sources with humans.

So, what can you do?

By educating the next generation on ways to preserve natural habitats, we set a strong foundation for a healthy future. Helping conservation efforts is a big step in the right direction. Organizations, such as Last Chance Forever out of San Antonio, Texas, make it their mission to rescue sick and injured birds. When possible, these birds are released back into the wild. Many other such organizations exist throughout the country and with the help of an informed and caring public, birds of prey may just have a chance.

If you'd like more information on Last Chance Forever, I encourage you to visit their site. http://www.lastchanceforever.org/index.asp

Works Cited:
"Birds of Prey." *Idaho Public Television*. N.p., 20 April, 2004. Web. 19 Sept. 2013. Retrieved from http://idahoptv.org/dialogue4kids/season5/boprey/threats.cfm

Timber's Gambit
Nature's Guardians Series Book 2
(excerpt)

I was born into a large and boisterous family with two brothers and three sisters.   My mother and father were the leaders of our pack. My father, a great alpha with obsidian fur, boasted that our pack was the largest in all the world. In my innocence, I believed him. My mother would sigh and roll her head, but my father would just puff out his chest and raise his chin. At night, with the pack gathered around the den, it was easy to believe my father's claims. Dozens of my kin lay scattered over the rocky ledges, spilling into the valley below. This was my favorite time of day. One by one, they would lift their heads to the sky, starting with my father, and sing out a chorus to the stars. The tiny voices of me and my siblings were drowned out by the multitude, but I knew one day, I would sing louder than all the others.

My sister Zoe and I always engaged in fierce competition. I wouldn't admit it, but her strength exceeded mine. Our other siblings found humor in seeing me pinned beneath her. At least she didn't gloat as some of the older wolves did. In fact, she often tried to protect me against their bullying. One such case ended with the intervention of our father, and my ultimate shame.

"Just because you're bigger, Thor, it doesn't mean you can push Timber around," Zoe said, the hackles on her back raised into spikes. "Don't you know he is the heir to the pack? You should show some respect!"

The other wolf, a gangly sandy youth barely one turn of the seasons old, paused for a moment before throwing his head back and laughing. His friends, born in the same season, laughed with him.

"There is no way Timber's going to be alpha," he said, turning golden eyes on her.

"How can you say that?" she snapped. "He is directly descended from the greatest alpha in all the land. You're just jealous!"

Thor lunged at her, snapping his teeth inches from her nose. She whimpered on instinct and cowered to the ground, pulling her ears close to her head. Thor continued to snarl at her, flashing his teeth and growling low in his throat.

"You don't know anything, she-pup," he said, his voice low in warning. "Don't you know that most of the wolves in the pack are directly descended from Zeus? Timber is just the most recent. The chances of him being the new alpha are slimmer than mine."

Regaining some of her courage, Zoe lifted her head. "If that is so, how come you have a better chance?"

"Because, sweet, innocent, naive Zoe, Zeus isn't my father. Nor is your mother mine."

Both Zoe and I gasped, understanding his meaning. Thor's mother had a forbidden meeting with a wolf outside of the pack. We weren't related in any way.

"Zeus could have banished my mother and abandoned us to the wilderness, but he pitied her. Lucky me."

He sat back on his haunches and raised his chin. I followed his example, not liking the way he looked down on me. His silent glare spoke of his resentment for me and my family. I couldn't understand where his hostility came from. Wasn't he grateful that father allowed them to stay in the pack, despite his mother's indiscretion?

"Know this, Timber," Thor continued, cocking his head to the side. "There is a long line of successors before you. If you really want to be an alpha, you are going to have to find a pack of your own. Zeus is not going to step down and even if he did, someone older than you will take his place."

"You mean, I have to leave?" I asked, horrified.

"Yes. I see Zeus' fire in you. This pack will not be able to tame the spark that is growing inside of you."

"But I don't want to leave."

"You will when you hear the moon calling to you."

"Stop it, Thor!" Zoe said, blocking me from his view. "Stop putting nonsense into his head."

"Well, as long as he has a girl to look after him, you don't have anything to worry about, Zoe," he said, getting to his feet.

"Wait a minute," I called, embarrassed. "I don't need her to protect me."

"Of course not."

Before I even realized what I was doing, I lunged at him, latching my tiny, needle-sharp teeth onto his leg. Thor howled, more in anger than pain. He reached down and grabbed me by my scruff. I released his leg and turned my head to snap at him, whining and growling at the same time. My mother was the only one to ever pick me up by my scruff and the indignity of Thor doing so was a blow to my pride. In his anger, he flung me away. I landed hard and rolled into a boulder, twisting my foot painfully. That was when my father came, alerted by my cries.

"Thor!" he bellowed.

The young wolf, as well as all those around him, coward low to the ground, some even turning onto their backs in submission. A high-pitched whimper issued from Thor and for one moment, I felt sorry for him. My father, head held high, towered over him, glaring down with his golden eyes.

"You dare attack a cub?" father said, his voice deceptively calm.

"No sir, I was only defending myself." Thor refused to look at my father, his gaze trained on the ground.

"Are you so weak to be threatened by a cub?"

"I'm sorry. It won't happen again."

"See that it doesn't."

"Yes, sir."

As soon as my father turned away, Thor and his followers fled for the trees. Father turned his disapproving glare onto me, and I shivered. With a sigh, he dropped his gaze and lowered his head. With the worst passed, I crawled to him on my belly, whimpering the whole way.

"Timber, are you all right, son?" he asked, nudging me with his nose.

"Yes, Father," I said, licking his nose.

"What am I going to do with you? I see so much of myself in you that it scares me."

He sighed again and laid down beside me. I snuggled into his fur for warmth and comfort.

"Stay clear of Thor. He is young and rash, and while I don't think he would really hurt you, it's better if you don't antagonize him."

"Antagonize?"

"Make him angry for no real reason."

"Yes, Father."

He glanced up at Zoe who sat a few feet away, staring at the place Thor had disappeared. Even from behind, I could tell she was still seething.

"Zoe," father called softly.

She turned her head around without moving the rest of her body. I noticed her body relax as she looked at us.

"Come here," he commanded.

She stood and turned around, loping over to us.

"I can't believe him!" she spouted, shaking her head.

"Don't think on it anymore," Father said, making room for her next to me.

My mind wandered from her and her outrage to the things Thor had said. Leave the pack? I would

never see my family again. Did I want that? I
pushed the troubling thoughts aside and tucked my
nose into my father's fur.

Also Available:

This collector set includes an autographed copy of the book, a collectable falcon from Wild Republic w/ authentic bird calls, and an adoption certificate.

Collection can be purchased on the Nature's Guardians website:

www.NaturesGuardiansBookSeries.com

Timber's Gambit

Young Timber is a grey wolf born into the largest pack in North America. Growing up as son to the great alpha, Zeus, he has the respect of the entire pack. However, after he causes a much-needed hunt to fail, Zeus convinces him to find a pack of his own. Facing mountain lions, rival wolf packs, humans, and a bullying coyote, Timber treks out across an unforgiving wilderness in search of the companionship and protection of a pack of his own. Find out what happens when his journey leads him into forbidden territory and humans come hunting for wolves!

Sahara's Plight

Growing up on the plains of Africa is anything but easy. Sahara faces lions, poachers, and an encroaching human population. With space a limited resource, Sahara must fight tooth and nail to survive the harsh African wilderness.

The *Sahara's Plight* collection set includes an autographed copy of the book, an 8" collectable plush (through Wild Republic), and an adoption certificate.

"Preserving nature one species at a time."

About the Author

Alisha M. Risen-Kent lives at home with her four children and cat in Texas where she loves working in her garden. Her passions are reading, writing, drawing, gardening, and photography and creates all the artwork for her books. She is also an avid player of Dungeons & Dragons© and comes up with most of her story ideas from the campaigns she plays in. An advocate for conservation efforts, she often volunteers where she can to help rehabilitate injured animals. She is also strong in her faith and believes that God has a plan for everything.

www.ingramcontent.com/pod-product-compliance
Lightning Source LLC
Chambersburg PA
CBHW030540290526
45786CB00004B/1791